Lease Options Made Easy

Vol. 1

Buying a Home with Little, No, or Bad Credit

Kevin A. Dunlap

Lease Options Made Easy: Vol. 1 – Buying a Home with Little, No, or Bad Credit

Copyright © 2015, 2017 by Kevin A. Dunlap
All rights reserved.

This publication is designed to provide competent and reliable information regarding the subject matter covered. However, it is sold with the understanding that the author and publisher are not engaged in rendering legal, financial, or other professional advice. Laws and practices often vary from state to state and if legal or other expert assistance is required, the services of a professional should be sought. The author specifically disclaim any liability that is incurred from the use or application of the contents of this book.

ISBN-13: 978-1505850598
ISBN-10: 150850592

This book is self-published.

Printed in the United States of America

Second edition

Dedication

This book is dedicated to my close friends who backed me regardless if times were affluent or tough. Thank you Necole, Ellie, Silvia, Kathleen, Russ, Wendy, Mike, my two brothers Kenneth and Kyle, and of course my father. Love you all.

Acknowledgement

I want to acknowledge some of the people who without their support over the last few years that this first book would never have been created.

First on the list is Lisa Sasevich. After hearing her talk to me about creating a book and the need to get my thoughts out to the world I realized just how much I needed to do this. Without your words this book would never have been created.

*I must also thank the following people for their advice in writing a book. Justin Runde (*Identity Theft Protection: How to Protect Yourself and Your Business*), Mai Lieu (*Take The Next Step: Secrets to Creating Success and Manifesting Your Dreams*), and Kathleen Petrone (*Confidence is Key! 12 Amazing Ways Public Speaking Empowers Your Child*) this final edition would never have been created.*

And to the last person just mentioned, Kathleen Petrone, you are the last and final inspiration to me. Without her initial encouragement and advice I never would have thought it was possible to become a published author. Thank you.

Also, to the people who helped me create a business for over 10 years in the lease option industry that has helped me create a living but more importantly allowing me to help others create the American dream of home ownership. First, thanks goes to Michelle Larson my first

Realtor® partner. Without starting that first business back in 2004-05 I wouldn't be here today.

Also, a special thanks to Mesha Graham. Without your help and continuation of this business I would be a far different man.

Also I want to thank Jim Eagan. After many years of partnership I am glad we made the original connection so long ago. Your friendship and business partnership has helped me grow over the years.

Investors like Glenn Plantone, John Rana, Girish Jashnani, Patrick Hickey, Brian Ferguson, Diana Dinninio, and so many others. Without you participating in my lease option program and willing to open up your investment homes there is no way I could have completed the types of deals to help so many people to become home owners.

My real estate broker, Glenn Plantone, also being open minded to allowing me to continue my lease option business after obtaining my Realtor® license has been immeasurable.

And of course I cannot forget my dearest friend of many years. My buddy, confidant, helper, and person who has supported me through thick and then. Thank you Necole Zeigler! Your love and support is greatly treasured.

I love you all. Thank you from the bottom of my heart.

Introduction

This book is intended to bring you the reader information on a unique way to purchase a home. This book is written from the viewpoint of a tenant who wants to purchase a home (thereby called a tenant/buyer) via a lease option program.

Any references in the second person, (e.g., you or your) is from the perspective as you are the tenant/buyer or the participant in a lease option program in which you are the one who wants to buy a home for you and your family. If you happen to be reading this from an owner or investor perspective please be aware of this nuance. Vol. 2, and Vol. 3 (i.e., later books) will be written from both of those perspectives, respectively.

It is the author's belief that people best learn from stories and the involvements which other people experience. Fictional characters were created so you can interact and to identify with people who are in the same situation as the intended reader of this book. In this volume/book you will be introduced to a couple named Roger & Peggy. They have challenged credit and want to own a home again but since they have challenged credit they will learn about lease options and how this can help them to become a homeowner. Many of the questions and techniques covered in this book

Introduction

can happen in your area regardless of city, state, or possibly even country.

We will also meet Derek & Sue. These two are owners of multiple real estate homes. They are briefly introduced in this book, Vol. 1. These two are the landlord/sellers of the story. And you will begin to get an understanding of lease options from their viewpoint. Vol. 2 will go a lot more into depth of the lease option from an Owner or landlord/seller perspective.

The third person we will be introduced to is Anthony. He is an investor (as we will go into a lot more detail on in Vol. 3) that specializes in creative real estate investing. He is also the one which will be giving a workshop that the main characters Roger & Peggy will attend.

I hope this book helps you in finding your next home.

Table of Contents

Chapter 1 – Introduction 3
Chapter 2 – What is a Lease Option 13
Chapter 3 – The Option Payment 17
Chapter 4 – The Rental Credit 25
Chapter 5 – Establishing the Purchase Price 37
Chapter 6 – Setting the Duration 53
Chapter 7 – Your Credit and You 61
Chapter 8 – Picking a Home 69
Chapter 9 – Qualifying & Terms 77
Chapter 10 – Exercising Your Option 97
Chapter 11 – Using a Realtor 105
Chapter 12 – Pros and Cons 109
Appendix A – About the Author .... Appendix i

Lease Options Made Easy – Vol. 1

Chapter
1

Introduction

In 2007 many areas of the US started to get hit hard by the real estate shift as housing prices began to drop. Many people faced foreclosure and thus many people lost their homes to the bank. Many others did a short sale on their homes which simply means that they sold their home for less than what they owed on the home. Quite a few of these previous home owners did not want to just rent a home or a room somewhere. Thus, the idea of lease option started to become a lot more popular.

In this book we will cover the concept of a lease option and how you as the tenant/buyer can get back on the path to home ownership and own a home again.

However, this book is not just written for the previous homeowner. If you have never owned a home before you can still benefit from this technique. This technique does not care if you have owned a home before. It does not care if you have good or bad credit. It doesn't even care how long you have been at your current job. And it doesn't even care how long you have been in the area or not.

One of the best growing trends today is for people to start doing a *lease option* on a home. Let's say we have a young couple named Peggy & Roger. Peggy and Roger are a couple that have only been married for 4 years and are starting to plan on raising a family and also want to buy a home. They are currently renting a 1 bedroom condo. Peggy is a nurse at a local medical clinic and Roger is a high school science teacher. They make pretty good money. However, Roger lost a home to foreclosure two years ago when the economy dropped in which his home lost nearly 50% of its value. Since they are married to qualify for a loan they will need both incomes. Even though Peggy has fairly good credit but Roger has bad credit.

Late one Friday night while Roger and Peggy were watching a movie there was a brief 30 second commercial about an upcoming half-day free seminar on *buying a home with little, no, or bad credit.* The host on the program, an investor called Anthony, was showing examples of people buying a home with this type of program and real live people getting the keys to their home.

They decided why not. It was free. And if they didn't like what was being said they would just leave. Roger called the number on the TV ad and made the reservation for the upcoming workshop. After hanging up the phone Roger turned to his lovely wife and said, "Honey, I think this is going to be great." She smiled back at him with a comforting smile.

As the day the Workshop approached Roger was getting very excited about the possibilities of owning a home again. Peggy was already starting to fantasize about a baby's room and having a bigger place rather than there cramped one bedroom apartment they were renting.

They drove up to the office that the workshop was being held just after noon on one Sunday afternoon. The Workshop was scheduled to open registration at 12:30 and begin at 1:00. To their surprise they saw a small crowd of people bustling to get inside.

> Roger looked over at his wife stating, "Wow! I did not know there were so many people who are in the same predicament as us."
>
> Peggy returned, "I know a lot of people who have been hurt by this housing crunch. I think there are a lot more people out there that may not even know that solutions like this could exist."
>
> Roger then returned, "I think you are right. I should have called my friend Mike. I never even thought about that."

They grabbed each other's hand and walked into the building.

On the whole way in Roger could not get out of his mind just how much the local economy was hurt by the downturn of the housing market.

Peggy, on the other hand, was thinking if there are this many people needing homes will there be enough to go around. You see Peggy was suffering from an ailment known as scarcity consciousness.

As they lined up to go into the event the line moved fairly quickly. There were three assistants in similar colored black T-shirts that read "Buying a home with little, no, or bad credit" on the back and "Homes Dunn Right!" on the front. The assistants were very friendly just taking some basic information from them, giving them a workbook, and name tags.

Peggy & Roger entered the conference room and saw that there were about 100 other people at the event. Soft classical music was playing that was very soothing and nice to the ear. They saw two open seats that were together and sat down in the third row.

Promptly at 1:00 of the assistants that checked them in came to the front of the room and announced:

"Good afternoon ladies and gentlemen. My name is Arlene. You may have seen me out front at registration. I want to thank you to our *Home Buying Easy Workshop* this afternoon. And in a moment our host Anthony Dunn will come out and show you how you can buy a home with little, no, or bad credit."

"I also want to acknowledge everyone for taking their time off this Sunday afternoon to spend a few hours with us. It is a great honor for us for you showing up today. It has been said that 90% of the reason why people succeed in life is just because they just showed up. What did I say? They just ...."

Everyone in the room excitedly announced "just showed up!"

Arlene continued with a smile, "That's right! Thank you. They just showed up. You see just three short years ago I too had bad credit. Terrible divorce completely ruined my credit. Then I found Anthony Dunn at a local book signing and he told me about his book on a subject called Lease Options. And then within four months I was in his lease option program. One and a half years later I am now a home owner of a beautiful home here in Las Vegas. It has been an incredible journey."

While she turned to her left and extending out her arm, Arlene announced "And without any further delay let me introduce you to the guest of honor today. My friend, my boss, and my savior…. Mr. Anthony Dunn." She began to applause which caused the entire room to also applause.

Anthony Dunn slowly jogged onto the stage and thanked Arlene with a handshake and a respectful bow which she returned also.

Anthony turned to the audience while Arlene started to leave the stage. He scanned the audience briefly and announced in a strong proud voice. "Everyone! Let's all give a hand for Arlene today. Wasn't she great? That is only her second time on stage. And this is her biggest audience." Everyone turned to Arlene to start applauding and her face shot beat red with pride and embarrassment all at the same time.

Then Anthony chirped up and stated, "Let's give yourselves a round of applause for taking the time out to be here today." The applause continued. After a few moments went by, "Thank you everyone. Thank you. As you may have already surmised my name is Anthony Dunn. I am a real estate investor for 15 years.

Wow, time sure does fly by. Well, I have been investing in real estate for 15 years now and about 10 years ago, before the housing crunch, I began to see a need for people that may not be able to qualify for a home to help them into getting a home. And that is what you will learn about today. Are you okay with learning on how to become a homeowner?" he asked raising his hand.

Almost everyone in the room raised their hand with a Yes response.

He continued, "Let me ask you this question. I am only asking this so I can see where we stand in this room today. Is it okay for me to ask you a couple of questions?"

Everyone yelled "Yes."

He continued, "Thank you. Let me ask you this. How many of you have owned a own home at some time in the past?" Roger quickly raised his hand. Peggy looked at him remembering the time he lost his home was early in their marriage. He had owned it for over 7 years. She remembered the dread he went through when the market crashed just so few months ago. Roger, on the other hand was dreaming of ownership. He was thinking oh my goodness this could be a way to own my own home again.

Anthony continued, "Thank you. How many of you own a home now? It could be that you own it free and clear, or that you may have missed a few payments or that you are doing a short sale, or even just have a current mortgage. So, by the raising of hands how many of you own your own home now?" About 15 people raised their hands. "Thank you. That is about average that I see. About 10% of the room owns currently and about 30 to 40% have owned before. So, I can get an accurate account how many of you have never owned a home before by the show of hands?" Peggy half raised her hand and so did a few other people. "Thank you. I appreciate your honesty. Today is your lucky day. It doesn't matter if you have never owned a home, or that you own a home now, or that you owned a home at some time in the past. Today you are going to learn how to get into another home that you are intending on buying in the near future."

Anthony continued by introducing a concept known as a **lease option**. And that is the sole topic of this book. It is to teach you the reader the pros and cons of doing a lease option on a home. Also, what to look out for and what to expect. This book is put together from mover a decade of experience specializing with the lease option strategy since 2004. I first heard about them when I bought my first investment property back in 2002. And I have put together hundreds of these and have seen so many different situations come up from doing them.

I recall talking with my first broker/agent about the lease option and she wasn't too thrilled to talk about it too much. This was back in 2002 when I was buying my first few homes in North Carolina. Two years later I then learned that most Realtors are not too keen on lease options for a few reasons. First and foremost they don't understand them. And secondly, they don't know how to make a commission on them so they tend to turn them away automatically.

In later chapters we will discuss these different strategies. And if you happen to be dealing with a real estate agent you may want to hand them a copy of this book and tell them to read it too.

Lease Options Made Easy – Vol. 1

Chapter 2

What is a Lease Option?

As related in the first chapter with Roger and Peggy a lease option is normally a program to help people that may not be able to qualify for a home to get into a home that they eventually want to purchase. Essentially you are buying a right to buy.

You can see something very similar in the stock market with option trading. In option trading you are either buying the right to purchase a particular stock or you are buying the right to sell a particular stock over a particular time frame. In real estate you are buying the right to purchase a home over a particular time frame.

You may ask 'What is the advantage of that to a buyer?' Well, let's look at this from this point of view. Let's say you know that your credit is going to be bad for say another 1 year. As an example you lost your home to foreclosure (much like Roger) about 3 years ago. You know current loan standards stipulate that you must wait at least 3 to 4 years before you can qualify for a loan.

Plus, you don't want to keep moving all of the time. You don't want to keep living in the current residence you are in because of whatever reason. Your family is growing. Or, the crime rate is on an increase in your current area. Or, you must relocate due to job transfer. Whatever the reason you just don't want to live in the place you are now and you want to buy soon and you don't want to move twice. Then something like a lease option is perfect for you. You can move into a home with this lease option and then within a year you are buying the home that you are currently renting.

Then when it comes time to purchase you simply do what is called "exercising your right to buy" or also known as "exercising the lease option". Depending upon the state you are in you will begin the buying process by opening escrow. This may be with a title company (typically the western have of the US) or a real estate attorney (typically the east part of the US). Your local mortgage lender will be able to direct you with that or just ask any Realtor you may know.

In your lease option you will have all of the terms already spelled out in the contract you signed at the beginning, which we will cover in a later chapter. To be brief there are 4 main terms that you will have in the contract will be the purchase price.

    1.) One is the price of the home. (Covered in Chapter 5.) This may be at a set amount or may be related to some market condition at the time you are exercising your right.

2.) Also you may have an option payment which is a payment you made at the beginning of your option to get into the home or to buy the right to buy (Covered in Chapter 3).

3.) Another is a rental credit which would be the amount each month that is applied toward the purchase. (Covered in Chapter 4)

4.) And last will be the time frame in which you can buy. (Covered in Chapter 6) There will be a specific start and end date. You will only be able to buy during those times unless you have a signed agreement to go beyond those dates.

Getting back to Peggy & Roger's attendance at the real estate workshop let's see how things went for them.

> As Anthony continued on with his presentation both Roger and Peggy were enthralled. Most of the rest of the attendees were eagerly listening.
>
> Anthony continued by asking "Before we get too involved with the mechanics of a lease option we do need to discuss some of the terms that you will need to become very familiar. A lease option has four main parts that need to be negotiated on any home. Three of them are financial agreements and the fourth is a time agreement. Let's get started."

Lease Options Made Easy – Vol. 1

Chapter
3

The Option Payment

Anthony continued, "One of the first things that we are going to look at is what is known as the option payment. You see the option payment is a one-time payment you make at the beginning of a lease option contract. It is what secures your right to buy the home."

Someone in the audience raised their hand and asked "How much is an option payment?"

Anthony turned around and looked quickly at the woman's nametag and said, "Good question Margaret. We are just about to cover that."

Anthony continued, "The option payment is normally paid at the beginning of signing the contracts. It is the part that secures your right to buy the home. It is also normally fully applied toward the purchase of the home. It is like a down payment, but different. A down payment is when you are actually purchasing the home.

The option payment is buying the right to purchase the home and can be converted to a down payment when you are actually getting ready to purchase the home with cash or a loan of some type."

Roger raised his hand and asked, "So the option payment is not the down payment."

Anthony said, "Good question Roger. Not at first. When you are starting a lease option on a home you are buying a right to purchase that home and the consideration or money that you are paying is legally binding the owner to sell you his right to sell the home. However, when you are ready to buy then that option payment is converted to a down payment toward the purchase. You see a down payment is when you are actually purchasing a home."

Roger replied "Ok. I think I get it."

Anthony smiled and quickly stated, "Thank you Roger for an excellent question. Everyone give Roger a round of applause." Which the rest of the audience did.

"Now Margaret asked a few moments ago about how much should you put down as an option payment? Well, that is very dependent on many things. Sometimes this will depend on the location of the home. Is it in an affluent neighborhood? Or a middle-class neighborhood? Also, the desirability to other amenities. For example is it a beach front home on the coast of San Diego? Or a home in the suburbs? Many factors go into the pricing of the option payment. And lastly what does the local market dictate? A lease option on a home in Birmingham will be different than a home in Los Angeles. Typically, without taking into account an average home you will typically see that the option payment ranges between 2 -5% of the overall value of the home. Thus, an average $200,000 home in Las Vegas would typically run around $4,000 - $6,000."

"Does that answer your question Margaret?"

She nodded.

"Now, I did mention before that the option payment can be converted into your down payment. Does everyone remember me stating that a few moments ago?"

Everyone nodded affirmatively.

"Well," Anthony continued, "that is not actually true. And it may not even be in your best interest to do that anyway." He paused to really let it sink in. "You see the option payment is money you CAN use as your down payment but it may not be best applied there. Has anyone heard of closing costs? Those costs for title companies to do their work. The costs for appraisals. The other costs it takes to close on your loan. Has anyone heard of those costs?" Anthony asked raising his hand.

Everyone also raised their hand shaking their head yes.

"Good. Now what if you could use that option payment to cover some or all of that cost too? Thus, reducing the money it takes for you to actually close on the loan. What if all the option payment and another payment you will be making monthly? What if you could use all of that toward your down payment AND your closing cost? How does that sound? Pretty good, huh?"

Peggy and Roger looked at each other and smiled. Wow, they could become a home owner possibly sooner than they had once realized.

"You see when you put down the additional funds like the option payment and rent credits – which we will cover later today – these can be used as a seller concession. Most cities and states allow the seller to pay some or all of the closing costs as well as down payments and even some other costs too. Well the option payment and rent credits are just that for you. They are seller concessions."

Peggy quickly asked aloud, "Is there a maximum amount that the seller can give back?"

Anthony acknowledged Peggy with a smile and said, "Yes. There is a limit. Good question. That limit will be restricted by either state or local laws or will be a limit by the bank you are using to get your loan."

Peggy intriguingly then asked, "What if I put more money down in that option payment and the rent credits you mentioned that the bank would not allow. I mean, what if I have paid $7,000 and the bank will only allow $6,000?"

"Great question. Who else in the room has a question or thought about that one?"

A few people raised their hands.

Anthony continued, "Thank you. Well Peggy you see you are always protected in the funds you put down. You can apply your funds toward your down payment. You can also have seller concessions. What if you still have more left over, well that can be used to reduce the actual purchase price. Using your example what if you paid $7,000 and can only use $6,000." Anthony turned to an easel holding a flipchart on it and started to write numbers on it..

"Let's assume for simplicity as these are not actual numbers that you are buying a $100,000. $3,000 is going toward the down payment and $3,000 is going toward closing costs. Everyone with me so far? The down payment comes off the actual purchase of the home. Thus, you would normally be getting a $97,000 loan. But what about the $1,000 you over paid? Do you see that instead of buying the home at $100,000 that the additional $1,000 can bring the purchase price of the home down to $99,000? Then the $3,000 down payment is included making it a $96,000 loan? Is everyone with me on this? You don't lose your money. It is just applied in another area."

Anthony turned to face Peggy and asked "Did that answer your question sufficiently?"

She smiled and nodded yes.

He then faced the rest of the crowd, "Did everyone understand this?"

Everyone nodded.

"Great. Everybody give Peggy a round of applause for asking a question that many of you had on your mind." Everyone applauded. Peggy smiled and sat down.

Roger, being very proud of his wife who doesn't normally stand up in these types of situations. "Great way to voice yourself, Honey." She smiled.

"Next we are going to go into the second financial part of a lease option. The Rent Credit."

As we have learned from the above example from Anthony's workshop the first of the financial elements of a lease option is the **option payment**. It is a one-time payment that a tenant/buyer uses to secure the right to purchase a home. This payment is usually paid at the onset of the agreement at the time the contracts are signed. Sometimes the landlord/seller will take this in installment payments if the amount is significantly large.

I have personally seen option payments in the $20,000 or more range. In some of those cases the owner has allowed to make the payments in smaller installments like $10,000 upfront and the remaining $10,000 to be paid in monthly installments from 1 to 3 or even 4 months. Every contract is different and the amount and how payments are made depend on what you as the tenant/buyer agrees to with the landlord/seller.

Chapter

4

The Rent Credit

In this chapter we are going to cover the second financial aspect of a lease option. This is known as the **Rent Credit**. Not every contract will have one of these attached. It will always vary depending on state or local restrictions as well as what the landlord/owner and tenant/buyer can agree upon.

Essentially the rental credit is simply the portion of each month's rent that is also applied toward the purchase of the home. This can be a small amount or can be significant. Typically you will see $200 - $300 per month being applied. I have seen as little as $0 credit (thereby keeping rents very low) and as high as $2000 out of a $2400 a month payment. Now these ranges can vary significantly.

Also, any rent credits that you receive will also be applied toward the purchase of the home. As Anthony mentioned in the previous chapter these can be applied in any of a number of ways. Ranging from lowering the purchase price, used as part of the down payment, or used as part of the Seller concessions toward your closing costs.

Let's see how Anthony explains this to the workshop that Peggy and Roger are attending.

> Anthony turns the page on the flipchart and begins to write RENT CREDIT on the flipchart with his body covering up what he is writing. He then turns away and asks the crowd.
>
> "What does that say on the flipchart?"
>
> The class in unison say "Rent Credit!"
>
> "Thank you. That is correct. We are now going to cover the rental credit. This rental credit is one of the most straightforward yet can also get to be a bit complicated parts of the lease option and is the second of three financial elements on a lease option."
>
> "The rental credit is simply how much money per month, if any, is being applied toward the purchase of a home. This money is the additional funds you will be paying at or above the normal rental rates for the home that you are in that will be applied toward the purchase of the home. Now, does everyone see why I am not using the word down payment here? That

your rent credit also goes toward the down payment?"

Peggy raised her hand again and stood up. "Is it because of the whole thing you just shared with us about the option payment can be applied toward the purchase, down payment, or closing costs?"

"Great answer Peggy. You are sharp!" Anthony said with a smile. "Does anyone else want to add anything to that?"

Roger raised his hand standing up next to his wife. "You said you had to be careful of the words we used. Thus, people may understand what we mean if you said 'down payment' but if I said that they would only assume the down payment part and not the other parts."

Anthony excitedly said, "Correct. Plus, there even could be a legal consequence for misusing the words. So yes you can say the rent credit could be applied toward the down payment or you can say it is being used toward the purchase of the home."

"Thank you Roger and Peggy. Give them a round of applause." Everyone did as they sat down.

"Let's talk a little bit more on the rental credit. Often times in a contract there are provisions that are included for what happens if you are late on a monthly rental payment. Some are quite strict and some are fairly lenient. The ones that I most often see is that if you happen to be late on a particular monthly payment then you may lose the rental credit for that month and just that month only. You are still paying the full amount you just may not be getting the credit for that month.

"Let me explain by an example." Flipping the page on the flipchart he begins to write down some numbers.

"Let's assume you moved into a home at the start of January. And you are paying $1300 per month and get a $200 credit. And let's say you are on vacation in July of that same year and forgot to pay July's rent until the 12th. Going by this example you are still paying the $1300 per month but you don't get July's rental credit. Let's say you buy the home at the end of December that year. How many months of rent did you pay?"

One person shouted out "12!"

"Correct! How many months of rental credit did you get in return?"

The same person shouted "11!"

"Correct! Does everyone understand the 1 missing month?"

Everyone nodded in agreement.

"Will this always occur this way? Anyone?"

Roger raised his hand and answered "Of course! That is in the contract."

Anthony responded, "Does anyone else want to answer that question?" with his arm held high.

Peggy hesitantly raised her hand.

Anthony, "Ok Peggy do you have a different viewpoint that Roger?"

Peggy slowly stood up and stated, "Well I have seen forgiveness on contracts. Once about a year ago Roger and I were visiting my sister in Vermont. We were gone for 2 weeks. It was in a pretty remote place and there were no banks around. I called my landlord and said I will be back on the 9th and was it okay to pay then. And he said that was no problem. Also, not to worry about the late fee since we always pay on time. You see, that was in our contract about the late fee and he forgave us on it. So, wouldn't an owner forgive or allow the rent credit to stay in place?"

Anthony responded, "Good answer Peggy. Does anyone else want to add anything?"

Another hand came up on the opposite side of the room from another gentleman.

Anthony: "Okay Carl what do you have to say."

Carl stood up and stated "There is almost always room for a temporary renegotiation of a contract. I would assume that would be here too. I mean, aren't landlords people too? I would guess as long as I wasn't always paying late or just stopped paying then the landlord could forgive a late payment or two. Right?!?"

Anthony: "Good answer Carl. You are close to what Peggy said too. And yes landlords are also people. They are family men and women. They go to church or help out in the community just like anyone else. In most cases if you call the landlord and say you are going to be late and you are not abusing this privilege then I don't see

Lease Options Made Easy – Vol. 1

why a landlord wouldn't forgive one or two late payments. And yes, Roger, a contract is a contract but also we are all human here. Things sometimes do come up." Anthony smiled at the knowledge these people were getting from his talk so far. "Thank you. Everybody give Roger, Peggy and Carl a round of applause for their questions and answers." Anthony and everybody applauded.

"Now let's review what we have learned so far. We start off by having an option payment that is due when you first sign the contract. You also have a monthly rental credit that you can get on a monthly basis. Over time like a year or even two this can become quite large. In an example let's say you put down $5,000 as an option payment. You also are getting $300 per month in rental credits. Over the course of say 20 months how much money would you have toward the purchase of the home, assuming no late payments?"

People started to scribble out their answers. A few people searched for their calculator app on their phones.

Anthony flipped a page on the flip chart and wrote out the math and then flipped a page to cover it up. After a few moments he again addressed the audience. "That should be about enough time. Who has an answer?"

Roger raised his hand and stood up with his notepad. "That is simply $5000 plus 20 times $300 or $6000. Wouldn't that make $11,000?"

Anthony flipped the page over on his flip chart which almost verbatim showed what Roger had just said. "That's right Roger $11,000. $11,000 would be applied toward the purchase of the home. Let's get a little more advanced here. Thank you Roger."

"Who in here knows what an FHA loan is and if so how much of a down payment you would require? Anyone?" Anthony asked widening his arms to encompass the entire room.

Carl from before shouted out. "It is 3.5% down payment, right?"

"Yes Carl. It is 3.5%. Good job. Let's do a little more math here. Let's assume you are buying a home worth $200,000. How much of a down payment is that?"

Carl whipped out his calculator and said "$7,000."

"Correct. Does everyone know how he got that answer? Or by the show of hands how many of you want to know how he got that answer?" About 7 people raised their hands.

"Thank you for your honesty. Here is how he got it. Thank you Carl you can sit down now." He scribbled on the flip chart $200,000 * 0.035 = $7,000

"Does everyone get that?"

Everyone shook their head.

"Great! Now let's go one step further. Let's go one step further. How much money do we have in this example going toward the purchase of the home?"

Peggy shouted out with 2 or 3 other people "$11,000."

"Correct. How much of that can be applied toward the down payment?" As Anthony points to the math he just did on the flip chart

Peggy again shouted with a few other people "$7,000."

"Correct again! Good job everyone. So how much does that leave for closing costs and could be applied toward the purchase price?"

Peggy again shouted "$4,000 Anthony."

"I love your spirit Peggy. You are correct for a third time." And Peggy smiled and got a little embarrassed. "Give Peggy a round of applause." Everyone did.

"That is correct. $11,000 was the total from the option payment and rental credits. $7,000 can be applied toward the purchase on a standard FHA loan. $4,000 more can be used for seller concessions toward the buyer's closing costs. Anything left over would go where…. Everybody?

Roger piped up this time saying "the purchase price of the home."

"Fantastic Roger. You are correct. Is everyone getting a good handle on this?"

So as you can see over the course of time you can be building up a sizeable payment that will be applied toward the eventual purchase of your home. Call or check with a local Realtor about estimated closing costs for your area. Typically around the nation a buyer's closing costs can run 2 – 3% of the purchase price of the home. Also, FHA guidelines on loans change so you want to call and check with your local loan officer on those regards.

Now that we have cover two of the financial elements in a lease option let's head into the third financial element and that is the Purchase Price…

Lease Options Made Easy – Vol. 1

Chapter 5

Establishing the Purchase Price

In this chapter we will be covering the **purchase price** of the home. On a lease option there are two main ways that a price is determined and agreed upon by both the landlord/seller and the tenant/buyer. Out of the two main ways a multitude of other possible ways could also be used to come up with the price, yet it is mainly a hybrid of the two main ways.

In my years of putting together lease options connecting landlord/sellers with tenant/buyers I have seen ways that are quite creative. We will cover some of those later in this chapter.

The most common practice in doing a lease option is to actually set a purchase price for the duration of the contract. Let's say you are doing a 2 year lease option. And both you and the landlord/seller agree that a fair price of the home is going to be $200,000. That is a locked in set price for the duration of the contract. If you bought it one day after starting the lease option then you are paying $200,000 (minus option payments, etc.). Or on the other hand you wait 24 months to purchase the price hasn't change a bit. It is still $200,000 (of course minus all of the option payments, rental credits, etc.). Thus, if you go off a set value then that is the price for the duration of the contract.

The second most common way to do a lease option is to have the price established at the time you purchase the home. This is called setting the price at the "appraised value at the time the option is exercised" or more simply "at the appraised value". You may ask how do you know what is that price? There are a small number of ways you can do this. The most common is to have a third party appraisal company go and appraise the home for you. This appraiser will establish value and report back to either the buyer or the seller (whomever hired him will get the report unless you go into it together). If both parties agree that the appraisal is a fair assessment of value then that becomes the purchase price and you move forward with the buying of the home. If one or both parties do not agree on this value then a second appraisal company can be hired to come out to assess value and then that one will be reviewed. Essentially one of three possibilities will occur.

      1.) You agree with the second appraiser and use that price.
      2.) You agree with the first appraiser and use that price.
      3.) You average the two appraisals together and use that price.

There are pros and cons which Anthony will get into in using either of the two methods.

> Anthony continued, "Now that we have covered all of the credits, then the next element to discuss is the actual purchase price of the home. This is not always as easy as it looks. Usually the landlord/seller wants the maximum price she can get and the tenant/buyer wants the lowest price that he can get. How does one decide on that? Also, what does the future hold since she may be selling the home up to 2 years (possibly even further) down the road?"
>
> "Let's now talk about the main two ways a price settled upon. They are as different as night and day. Both have some great benefits to either party. And both have some drastic negative aspects, too."
>
> "The two ways to determine price is going off a set price that is agreed upon today that will last the duration of the entire contract. Or you can go off the fair market value also called the appraised value at the time that you as the tenant/buyer exercise your option."

Roger raised his hand and asked "But isn't going off the set price better? That way you know exactly what will the price will be."

Anthony responded "Good question. However, that may not always be the best solution. It all depends upon what you think the market will do over the next one or two years."

Peggy mentioned aloud "Right, what if the market goes down in value or I think it will go down in value."

Anthony responded, "You hit the nail right on the head for the second way to establish price and that is to go off of the appraised value at the time you are ready to get a loan and purchase. In the industry we call this setting the price at the appraised value at the time the option is exercised."

"You may then ask which one is better? Which one is better for you the tenant/buyer and which is better for the landlord/seller? Am I right?"

The audience responded half confused yet still fully engaged.

"Okay, let's talk about some of the advantages and disadvantages of each. Most of these are going to depend on which way you see the local real estate market is trending in the near future."

"If you are the owner of the home and you see strong appreciation then you may want to go off the appraised value so that you gain as much of the value that you can. If you are unsure what the market will do in the future then you may want to set the price. Of course if you set the wrong price either too high or too low then that could hurt you too."

"Let's say you are the owner of a home and you set the price too low. For example you set it at $175,000 and the market goes up to $200,000 and the tenant exercises their option. They just gained $25,000 in equity that you missed out on by setting the price too low. Or what if you set the price too high. Let's say you thought the market would go very high and you set the price at $225,000. The market turned and only went to $190,000. Either you as the landlord/seller will have to renegotiate the terms with the tenant or stick to your agreed upon price."

"Then let's look at this from the tenant/buyer perspective. As Roger pointed out a few minutes ago isn't having a set value the best? I mean you know what your price is going to be beforehand, right? Well by setting the price you do know what the price very well could be. If you speculate the prices are going up strongly and you are able to set a price that is conservative then you may be walking away with some equity at the time you buy. This would be a big win for you. You get a home that already has more value than what you paid. However, the converse is also true. If you set a price that is too high and the value comes in lower then you only have a few options available to you."

"Let's review these since I know that your burning question before we talk about the second strategy."

"The options you have available to you if you set a price too high are:
First, talk and renegotiate with the landlord/seller on the terms. They may very well be willing to lower the price. As long as she has made a profit on the home they may be willing to go ahead and sell so that they can get cashed out to buy or invest in something else.
Second, you can see if they will be willing to extend the contract for more time to allow the market to appreciate to the higher price while keeping the price the same or possibly even lowered.

Third, there is always the possibility of asking and getting what is called Seller Financing. This is when the owner can be your bank either in full for the purchase amount or they can carry a second loan that will be placed to cover the difference between what your bank gives you and the remaining balance of the purchase price. Of course there are many, many more options available but these are the main three."

"I know I have covered a lot in these past few minutes. By a show of hands who, at least partially, understands what I have covered?"

Most people either raised their hand or partially raised their hands.

Anthony continued, "That is what I thought. Briefly we will review. Who in here has a question on going off of the set price?"

Roger raised his hand again and asked, "Okay I see there is some great advantages for doing a set price. The upside is that if I think the market is going to increase a lot over the next one or two years than I can try to get the price as low as possible? And.... If the market doesn't go up as much as I thought the worst case scenario is that I either have to renegotiate the price with the owner or extend the contract for more time?

That seems like something is a good possible risk where the big win is possible equity."

Anthony nodded "That is a great way to look at." More heads start to nod up and down from the rest of the audience. "Thank you Roger for making that clearer to everyone. Give Roger a round of applause."

Anthony continued on, "Now let's go over the pros and cons of the second strategy which is buying at the appraised value.

"Many of you may say this is the fairest way to go. You are buying based on the value at the time you are buying. This can be very fair. Both sides are taking the gamble that the future market will work in their favor. And buying at its value can be a huge advantage. However, there are some major disadvantages of that strategy too. What if you are moving into the home and it is worth $150,000 today and you prepared that by the time you buy the market would probably take it up to $175,000 and that is within your affordability range. Then let's say there is a spike in the local economy and the price jumps up to $225,000. Now you are way out of your budget. You can no longer afford to buy the home. Without some serious renegotiating with the owner then you may not be able to afford this home or even if you move out and try to buy another place locally you are not able to buy those homes either. Thus, you could lose.

"On the flip side let's say the local market tanks and the price goes down from $150,000 and drops to $110,000. Even though the owner still has to sell to you if you bought but what if they owe $140,000 and they don't have the cash to sell it to you. Then what? Possible a lengthy short sale or some other type of renegotiation.

"Even though the appraised value may seem the fairest way to go, it doesn't allow for big market changes. It works great in a market that is steadily increasing or is staying about the same."

Peggy chirped in asking "Wow, there is a lot to think about when we are coming up with the price."

Anthony turned to Peggy, "That's right Peggy. This is why it is important to know something about the area that you are buying. If you think the market will go up a lot then going off the set price may be best. If you think the market will only go up a little or even go down in prices then asking for appraised value would be best."

From the other side of the room Carl asked, "Is there any other strategy that isn't so dramatic?"

Anthony responded "Yes, there is and we will cover hybrid strategies next…"

As Anthony had mentioned there are ways that you can minimize risk to either or both parties of this transaction. Some of these are by setting caps on either the upper price or the minimum prices.

Some of the interesting ways I have also seen is to use a maximum or minimum value or both.

Hybrid Strategy 1: Appraised value with a Maximum Price

In a maximum value you may agree to go off the appraised value at the time the option is exercised yet set a maximum price of a specific dollar amount regardless if it appraises more than that or not. In this example let's say you are agreeing to the appraised value and set the price will go no higher than $200,000. Assume the value came in at $220,000. The purchase price is $200,000.

Then what would happen if the price came in at $180,000? We have already said it is at the appraised value with a maximum of $200,000. In this case then the price is $180,000.

When do you think we would use this strategy? This could be used when you are pre-qualifying for a loan and based on income your lender states you can go no higher than $200,000. This is an excellent strategy for that one. Also, some investor-owners could say that as long as they are getting the fair market value that they are okay at capping the price at a specific dollar amount like $200,000.

Hybrid Strategy 2: Appraised Value with a Minimum Price

In this scenario you still going off the appraised value at the time you exercise except this time there is a minimum capped value. This would look something like appraised value with a minimum of $150,000. This means that if the value came in over the amount then that is the price of the home. That is the fair market value. Thus, in this example if the appraised price was at $190,000 then the purchase price is $190,000.

What happens if the appraised value comes in at $130,000? Since there is a minimum value the purchase price would be $150,000 regardless of the appraised value below it.

Why would someone do this strategy? Usually this is more on the side of the landlord/seller. This may be what they still owe on the property or what they paid for it (or paid for it with a minimum amount of profit). Even though this is not necessarily to the benefit of you as the tenant/buyer it may be a requirement to do the deal.

I don't want you to get too concerned on this as you may already be thinking that you are being screwed automatically when seeing one of these. Typically the minimum value may be way below what the market is showing. Then this is more of an insurance type policy for the landlord/seller. Let's say that she bought the home a few years ago at $140,000. The market indicates a fair value today at $195,000. And you both agree to this strategy with a minimum price of $150,000. Unless the market tanks over the next one or two years this minimum value doesn't really even apply to you or would be of very little concern.

Hybrid Strategy 3: Appraised value with both a Minimum and Maximum Value

This is one I haven't seen too often in the years of doing lease options. However, it is a logical blend of both of the previous two strategies. This simply means a maximum price is set that you won't go over and a minimum price is also set. Ideally this is creating a target range for the price.

For example, you may be doing a contract with a minimum of $150,000 and a maximum of $200,000.

You will pay at least $150,000 for the home and not pay in excess of $200,000. If it appraises above the maximum price you have instant equity in the home. If it appraises for less you will still have to pay at least the minimum value.

Hybrid Strategy 4: Appraised Value with a Maximum Price and then Split the Difference

When I first started doing lease option in 2004 in Las Vegas the market was going through the roof. Nobody could predict how much home prices were going to soar over the next year, much less two (not even knowing of the real estate bust). This was the most common strategy we used for about 2 years. This strategy gives the investor or landlord/seller a maximum price that they are okay with but also left some money on the table for the tenant/buyer.

Here is a scenario from back in 2004. This can be seen in any market that is heavily appreciating.

A home is bought by an investor for $100,000. Market increases at that time was 50% or more per year. Thus, an investor could realistically just rent the home (not a lease option) and expect to sell it at $150,000 or more after 12 months. (More about the 12 month reason in our third book.)

However an investor could come in and do something like the following. Since appreciation of homes were skyrocketing and the tenant/buyer could still be left with some money or equity in the home a contract would go something like this:

Purchase price is set at $140,000 plus 50% of any difference above that number. Thus, if the price comes in below the $140,000 price then the price is $140,000. If the price comes in above that number then the price is mathematically calculated. Let's say the market did better than it may have looked like it did at the start of the contract. Let's say the value comes in at $180,000. The price would be $180,000 - $140,000 = $40,000 for the difference in the appraised and maximum price. That $40,000 would normally be split 50/50 thus making the difference $20,000. Adding this to the $140,000 would make a purchase price of $160,000. There is still $20,000 left on the table for the tenant/buyer as equity.

This was one strategy that was one of the more creative techniques I have seen. Of course they can be a lot more convoluted than just these four hybrid strategies and the two main strategies.

In the long run it doesn't matter which strategy that you use. So as long as both people are in agreement to the final outcome then it is fair to all parties.

Now that we have covered all three financial elements we have one more element in a lease option contract that needs to be addresses, and ironically TIME is of the essence…

Lease Options Made Easy – Vol. 1

Chapter 6

Setting the Duration of the Contract

We have covered the main three financial elements of a lease option contract. In a quick review these are:
1.) The option payment. This is the payment that secures your right to purchase
2.) The rent credit. This is the incentive the owner is giving you to pay on time and to purchase the month paid out of each of the monthly rental payments.
3.) The purchase price. Either by setting the price or going off of the appraised value at the time the option is exercised.

Now it is time to cover the duration of the contract. When does it begin? When does it end (how long is it)? And is there any restrictions on how soon you can buy?

Setting the time frame on the contract may be one of the most important aspects of the contract. Over the years I have seen contracts as short as 6 months or as long as 5 years. The duration of the contract is up to time that you and the landlord/seller agree to.

Since a lease option is also a form of rental ship most contracts usually begin at the start of a new month and end at the end of a month. Of course there is not a rule or something you must do. This is simply a guideline to keep things a little neater. As a rule of thumb the contracts that I have normally done begin at any time of the month that the tenant/buyer needs to move in yet I normally have them end at the end of a month.

Depending on what your local market is doing the length of a contract can be for any time. Normally I see 1 or 2 years for a contract. More times than not the tenant/buyer moving into a lease option home has poor or challenged credit and they need at least a year to get their credit repaired so that they can qualify for a loan.

Sometimes, and we will cover this more in the third book, there are reasons why a landlord/seller cannot sell a home for a specific period of time. Not to get too much into the details it can be a capital gains tax reason. So don't be surprised if there may be a year clause in a contract before you can purchase, especially if he just bought the home recently.

Another concern is how soon you want to move in after you have signed the contracts. Some people want to move in that same day and others require more time. I have seen as short as 2 hours and as long as 2 or more months. This is again dependent upon your needs and how long the owner is willing to wait. Typically it is 2 – 4 weeks from the signing of the contract until you actually getting the keys and moving in. Many people have to give notice to a current landlord and this is often 15 to 30 days' notice. I have even seen some people were staying in an extended stay hotel and had everything in a moving truck and needed a place the same day.

Let's return to Anthony's presentation.

> Anthony continued by saying, "Okay. Now that we have covered the three financial aspects of a lease option contract let's now get into one of the most important ones. The length of the contract. In my experience it is rare that a person who enters into a lease option contract that is not an investor will be able to buy in the first 6 to 12 months. Most people enter these with needing at least a year to get their credit in order so that they can buy."
>
> Someone in the audience asked, "What is the main reason they can't buy now?"
>
> Anthony quickly responded, "Great question. The reason can be just about anything. The most common ones are that they have recently lost a home to either foreclosure or sold their previous home through a process called a short sale.

Other reasons could be that they went through a bankruptcy recently. Possibly a divorce or a spouse or loved one went through a costly medical procedure or event. Regardless of the reason they recently went through a difficult time, namely financially which effected their credit. Essentially they just need time to get their credit in order to be able to buy again. Does that answer your question?"

The audience member nodded yes and sat down.

Roger turned to Peggy and said "That is me. I lost my home to foreclosure about 2 and a half years ago. This seems perfect for us."

Peggy nodded. She put her hand on his leg and smiled assuredly.

Anthony continued, "The duration of the lease option is open to negotiation. Normally they are at least 1 year, but I have seen ones go on for much longer. On residential homes you typically see between 1 and 3 years. On land and commercial types of deals these can go on for 10 or more years. And yes, you can do a lease option on just about any type of real estate. From land, to homes, to things like a casino or high rise building. However, today we are only going to talk about residential properties. Condos, townhouses, homes and manufactured homes."

"The length of the contract is crucial and also may have some restrictions. Some owners want to go as long as possible on the option and some are okay with buying at any time. You have to see what their restrictions are."

Roger quickly asked, "Why would an owner put a restriction on when you can buy? I mean don't they want to get cashed out sooner than later?"

Anthony responded, "In most cases they do want to get cashed out quickly. That way they can buy something else and do this all over again. However, there are owners that may have just recently purchased a home and they don't want to pay something like a 'short term capital gains tax'. This is a tax where they could be taxed two or three times the amount on the profit of an investment home if they sold that home in under 1 calendar year. Meaning if they sold the home at 365 days or less they would pay a lot more tax on it. If they waited until the 366th day or later they could be paying a lot less tax. Another reason is that maybe the profit margin is slim and they are wanting the cash flow from the rental to help adjust their bottom line. Does that make sense, Roger?"

Roger nodded and said, "I think I get it. The length of the contract depends upon the needs of both the tenant/buyer and the landlord/seller."

Anthony nodded and said, "You've got it down perfectly Roger. Does everyone else also understand this so far?" as he raised his hand in acknowledgement.

The audience all raised their hands in understanding.

"Perfect. Let's continue. Most residential homes go for 2 or 3 years. This should give ample time for just about anyone who is actively working on their credit to qualify. Let me say that again. This gives ample time for *anyone actively working on their credit to qualify for a loan.* The key words here is 'actively working on their credit.'"

"The biggest reason I see why someone doesn't buy is that they never worked on their credit to be able to buy. Working on your credit can be simply just paying all of your bills on time. If you lost your home to foreclosure and you simply paid all of your utility bills, your credit card bills, and car payments on time your credit would just naturally go up."

"And, eventually the weight of the hit from the foreclosure will subside as time goes by. The problem I see is that once people stop making a home payment they also start to develop other bad habits of not paying their other bills on time either. And over time they maintain that habit and thus never are able to raise their scores."

Peggy quickly asked, "Are there ways to raise your score besides making payments on time?"

And with that we will cover in the following chapter.

Chapter
7

Your Credit and You

The number one reason that I see why people do not exercise their option on buying a home is that they actually never took the measures to repair their credit. Quite frequently their credit may have become worse.

Some of the best ways to increase your score is simply to pay your bills on time. Also, tracking your score on a monthly basis from a site like www.myfico.com would be very advantageous. Other sites may also give scores but may not be as accurate as the aforementioned one. This is because they use their own approximation on the credit algorithm that MyFico actually uses and an approximation can have some errors.

Let's revisit the workshop with Peggy's last question to Anthony.

> Peggy quickly asked, "Are there ways to raise your score besides making payments on time?"

Anthony smiled and said, "I'm glad you asked Peggy. Yes there are ways to raise your scores. It takes a little time but you can do it and this is perfectly legal. Actually, not only is it legal it is highly recommended by many banks and credit unions."

"You see they want you to raise your score so that they can lend to you. That is how the banks and credit unions make their money. It is on the interest they collect on the money they loan to you. One novel little technique a lot of local credit unions do – not the major banks mind you – it is the local credit unions. They have programs out there where you can do an installment loan. What is it called again? An..."

Everyone chimed in, "an installment loan."

"Correct. An installment loan. An installment loan is a great way to increase your credit and it costs you very little money. You can even borrow the money from a friend and give it back to them at the end of the same day. How novel is that concept?"

Everyone looked at him in utter confusion.

Anthony smiled and continued, "An installment loan works like this. Check with your local credit union and see if they will allow this. Let's say you have or can borrow from a friend $2,000. You take that and maybe an extra $100 out of your pocket. You then go an open up a secured savings account. What is that again? A ..."

Everyone chimes in "Secured savings account."

"Correct! A secured savings account. That is what you talk to the bank employee about. You put in the $2,000 into that account. Now you are not able to touch that money because it is secured. You cannot withdraw it nor close the account. You tell the banker you would like to borrow $2,000 based upon the $2,000 in that secured account. The banker is happy because he knows that the loan he is giving to you is secured against that secured savings account."

"Here is the kicker. Some credit unions will allow you to make payments out of your secured savings account to pay down the balance of the loan. That is where the extra $100 or so comes in. You place that into little extra money into the secured savings account. This will cover the first payment and future interest payments which at this time would be very low, probably less than 4%! You take out the loan for 2 years... How long?"

Everyone chimed in again, "2 years!"

"Yes, 2 years. That is the optimal amount of time to do this. Now let me really make sure you understand this. You have placed $2,100 into a secured savings account. You borrow $2,000 of that and you set up automatic payments so that your savings account pays down your loan on a monthly basis. Thus, you are never actually even making a payment physically yourself. At the end of the 2 years which so happens to be the length of your option contract you have just built up a great trade line. Does everyone get this so far? We are just getting started here."

People raised their hands in acknowledgement.

"Now, let's make this really fun. Let's say you have $5,000 for an option payment to do a lease option on a home. Before you pay the $5,000 on the option payment, why not go ahead and use that money to put $2,000 into a secured savings account and borrowing the $2,000 back. If we ignore the interest money to help seed the monthly payment, do you see you still have the full $5,000 for your option payment?"

Everyone raised their hand in acknowledgement.

"Great! Now let's even go deeper into this technique. Would you all agree that if one installment loan looks good on your credit then how do two installment loans look? Do you think it would look better that you paid two off on your credit report?"

Everyone nodded in agreement.

"Are you following what I am about to say?"

Roger raised his hand and said, "Oh my goodness. You could do this 2, 3 or 100 times."

Anthony smiled and said, "Correct. The only limitation are going to be two factors. Number 1, the number of credit unions that are available that will allow you to do the secure savings account and to borrow money with preferably automatic payments and the second one is…. Roger do you want to take a stab at what that second one is?"

Roger thinking for a second replied, "Well wouldn't it get expensive in the interest payments? I mean, if I did this 100 times and I needed an extra $100 or $200 to pay the interest then that could cost be over $10,000."

"Correct. That is the second limitation. Even though we could almost ignore the $100 to $200 to seed the account for the automatic payment on the first account, if you did this 5 or even 10 times that could get costly. Thus, you would do this only the number of times you are willing to afford to do it."

Then Roger asked, "So when I am ready to find a home on lease option that is when I do this?"

Anthony, "Good question, but no."

Everyone in the room was shocked at this answer.

Roger said, "I shouldn't do this when I am ready to do a lease option on a home?"

Anthony returned, "No. The best time to do it is right now. Before you do a lease option on a home. You do it when you have the funds available or even partially available. If you wait until you are ready to do the lease option then all that time you spend looking for a home is wasted as far as your credit repair part goes. Let's say it takes you 2 months to find the perfect home and you had the money available the whole time. Do you see you could already be 2 months into the rebuilding your credit? That way you could possibly even buy earlier?"

Roger replied, "Wow! I never knew this could be so easy."

Anthony, "Not only is it easy and even legal. It is encouraged by the bank."

So as you can see from the important information Anthony is giving to the workshop attendees there are many ways a person can work on their credit.

These are just a few tricks you can do to boost your scores. Let's recap them and add in a few additional ones.

First you learned that simply paying all of your bills on time will boost your score over time.

Second any derogatory regardless if it is a small one like a late payment to a major one like a foreclosure or bankruptcy that over time these challenges become less important and will eventually just fall off your credit report.

Third, you can help rebuild your credit by doing an installment loan, preferably for 2 years.

Additional items is to make sure that if you do get new credit lines that they are Visa or MasterCard ones. You can go to websites like www.creditcards.com to apply for new credit cards regardless if you have excellent credit or poor credit. Some of them charge an annual fee and some do not. Use these and any credit card sparingly as usually the interest rates can be quite high. I would recommend keeping a small balance on them to show activity but keep it under the 25% usage limit. Anything above that can start to show negatively on your report.

Lastly, pull your credit at least once a year from www.myfico.com. This is the truest method to see your rate. You can even join their monitoring system for a fairly nominal price.

Look over your credit report, possibly with a credit repair expert and look for things on your report that are inaccurate. This can range from having a trade line that does not belong to you to inaccuracies in your personal information (name misspellings, wrong addresses, wrong employment, etc.) Even though some of these seem small the points do add up.

I hope this chapter in duration and also working on your credit was helpful. In the next chapter we will cover how to pick the best home for you.

Chapter 8

Picking a Home

Now that you understand the process, then what? You have already started working on your credit. You have the money available now all you have to do is find that perfect home. There are a multiple number of ways to finding that perfect home for you.

You must now go out and search for homes that a lease option is available on. There are Realtors who can help there and there are sometimes companies that specialize in lease option as a strategy. One way to search for them is to simply do an internet search for your local area. If nothing comes up then you may want to attend a local REIA (Real Estate Investment Association – www.reia.com) to find one. A lot of investors go to these meetings. Some of them may be keen to doing a lease option on some of their vacant homes. Others may know people who specialize in this strategy.

Once you find someone then it is looking for that ideal home for you. The number of homes available with a lease option is a small portion that is available out there. Less than 5% of any homes are seeking a lease option as a possibility. This by no means should dissuade you. Just because the number of available homes is small doesn't mean you are not able to find that perfect place. To start look at the homes where the owner has already expressed an interest in doing a lease option. If that doesn't work then you can (or have your Realtor) call the owners to see if they would be interested in doing this strategy. This could be a For Sale sign or a For Rent sign. A lease option is a hybrid of both. Especially call the owners that have both a For Sale sign AND a For Rent sign in the yard.

Let's assume you go to a local investment club meeting and you meek Derek & Sue. A husband and wife investment team. They buy homes, fix them up and then offers the homes either as a rental or more preferably as a lease with option to buy. We will cover their strategy in *Lease Options Made Easy Vol. 2* for the perspective of the landlord/seller. Suffice it to say that there are some great advantages to an owner.

> Roger and Peggy learned a lot at the workshop and found a local REIA meeting that is going to be happening tonight. It's been 6 weeks since they did the workshop. Peggy found a credit union that does the installment loan and she did exactly what Anthony had suggested. She took $2,000 out of their home buying account and

gave an extra $150 to be safe and opened the secured savings account and then borrowed against that account of $2,000 which she diligently placed back into their home buying account. She set up automatic payments to come from the $2,150 savings account so she does not have to do anything except open the mail once a month to verify all payments are going on properly.

Being very excited that they found a local REIA meeting Roger can barely restrain himself. He is speaking to his wife all about the possibilities. Peggy being a bit more reserved is hopeful that tonight things will go well at the meeting and that they would find someone there who can help.

They arrive 15 minutes prior to the meeting to find nearly 40 people there. Some are dressed very casually and others in suits (some with metal name tags on). She notices mortgage brokers, Realtors, and even a couple of insurance agents. Upon speaking to one person that is casually dressed she learns that he is a new investor still waiting to get his first deal done. So people at all levels of home buying come to these events.

Then they notice Anthony from the other week. And he recognizes Peggy and Roger. He makes his approach.

Anthony says, "Wow! It is good to see you two here. How have you been?"

Eagerly Roger shakes Anthony's hand, "Peggy and I are wonderful. You really helped open our eyes."

Peggy joined in, "We have been following your advice. We are working on the installment loan. We have also started talking with a mortgage broker. And this is our first investor function."

Anthony replied, "That is wonderful."

Roger chimed in, "And we are here to find investors who may be able to do lease options."

Anthony, "I think I know someone for you to meet. Right now I don't have anything for lease option that fit what you told me a couple of weeks ago. Let me introduce you to Derek and his wife Sue. They buy all kinds of homes and they do a lot of lease options. He called it their preferred "exit strategy".

Anthony led them across the room to another couple that was engaged in a conversation with another gentleman.

Anthony placed his hand on a man's shoulder and the man turned to greet him.

"Derek, how are you? I haven't seen you here in a couple of months."

Derek turns around and with a big smile and sturdy handshake, "Anthony! It's good to see you. Sue and I have been really busy. Four houses we are working on right now."

Peggy and Roger are actually shocked. They are working on four houses? They only need one.

Anthony continues, "Derek I want to introduce you to Roger and Peggy." He then turns to Roger, "And Roger... Peggy.... This is Derek and Sue."

Some handshakes and gratuities pass between the 5 people.

Derek then asks, "So are you two new in investing?"

Roger quickly interjects, "Oh, no, no. We aren't investors. We are actually wanting to become a homeowner again. Anthony here says you may have some lease option homes available."

Sue interjects, "We actually do. We are marketing 3 right now. What are you looking for? And how do you know about lease options?"

Peggy chimes in "We took this lease option workshop a few weeks ago…"

Sue, "Was that one of his workshops?" as she points to Anthony.

Peggy says, "Yes. It was quite good. It really got us excited about becoming a home owner again."

Sue, "Yes. He does a great job and has some great material." And smiles confidently at Anthony.

Derek interjects, "Let me show you what we have." He then opens up a binder with a few fliers with pictures on it and shows the homes to both Peggy and Roger. They thumb through the papers and got very excited on the last one.

Peggy turns to Roger and says, "Honey, I think this is it. It is the right price, the right side of town." She turns to Derek and asks, "This home is still available?"

Derek smiles and says "It is. We can look at it tonight if you want."

Roger and Peggy turn to each other and smiled.

Later that night the four of them were at the home touring through its features. Peggy and Roger fell in love with it. It was perfect for them. And the price and terms were exactly what they were expecting. They could not fathom just how easy the process was. If Anthony had not walked them through it at the workshop there would be no way that they could be on the path to homeownership.

After touring the home Derek brought out a lease option contract followed by a rental contract. The rental spelled out the terms of the 2 year rental. The lease option contract spelled out the terms of the purchase. Derek stated since he and Sue just bought the home a month ago that he could not sell the home for at least 11 more months for tax reasons. Thankfully, Roger and Peggy were already warned that this may occur. Roger and Peggy were already ok with this as he still had more months to wait to have the foreclosure on his credit no longer limit him from getting a loan.

They signed the paperwork that night. And agreed to meet up in the morning for payments. 30 days from now they would be moving into the home that they were intending on buying.

Chapter 9

Qualifying & Terms

You are in the home, now what?

Your next goal is getting qualified to purchase. Your first step is to start to interview local mortgage lenders or mortgage brokers. The difference between the two will be discussed shortly.

You should continue to work on credit issues. Both paying bills on time and seeking new lines of credit. One warning is not to overdo the new lines. That could be seen as a desperate measure on getting money and would show up as a red flag to any creditor.

Sometimes credit is just a waiting game. If you have pristine credit except for that foreclosure 1 year ago then you may have to wait until 3 or 4 years just because of the foreclosure.

If you have a lot of negative items then you may have to become good with those creditors or find ways to remove derogatory items from your credit report.

The process of qualifying for a loan and getting the loan may take some time. Start talking with a mortgage broker. You will also start to learn a new language with all of the terminology that will be tossed around. Let's go ahead and cover those so that you are familiar with these when you are at this step.

The rest of this chapter will be dealing with terms and they are grouped into their own sections. You can skip whichever parts that may not apply to you.

Mortgage broker vs. Mortgage lender

A <u>mortgage broker</u> is a person who can shop multitude of different conventional banks to find the best loan for you. While a <u>mortgage lender</u> is at a specific bank and can only show you the loans that specific banks has for you.

For example, you walk into Bank of America (let's say this is where your savings and checking account reside) and you speak with a *mortgage lender* for a home loan at that bank.

There are advantages to both. In the case of the mortgage broker that person will shop through an array of banks and, depending upon your credit score, pick a bank that has the best loan program for you. Thus, let's say your score has a middle score of 702. Bank A has a loan program for people with a 690 - 720 score where you can get a loan at an interest rate of 6.5%. Bank B has a similar program for people with a 690 - 720 score and only charges 6.25% (all other terms on the loan are exactly the same). Thus, the mortgage broker would say to you that Bank B has the best loan for you.

Now let's say you have a long-term history at Bank C. You have been there for two decades. You know the bank president pretty well. You see her about every once a week or two and you have very good rapport with her. Then comes the day that you want to purchase a home. You visit her and she looks over all of the loans her bank can offer. She knows you and she knows what terms her bank can offer. You realize that since you have had such a long-term relationship that the loans she can offer are quite competitive to other institutions. Plus, the personal relationship can go a long way if there are any restrictions or complications.

To determine which is best is to know the rapport you have with your current bank. If you feel you have a good connection with them, you may know some of the vice presidents, or you have a strong customer loyalty then the *mortgage lender* may be your best choice. If you want to "shop around" a bit then dealing with a general *mortgage broker* would be preferred. Both people are referenced by the word "lender". I know that may be a little confusing however that is just the way it is.

The main difference are the loan programs that are available and the personal interaction you may have with one institution. The mortgage broker has that access. She may be able to qualify you from one bank where a different bank would not qualify you or possibly give you less favorable terms. The reason you may want to use a mortgage lender at one bank is the personal relationship you may have developed and that can many times go a long way to qualifying you even though you technically may not qualify for a loan. In this writer's opinion I would suggest developing a relationship with the mortgage lender at the bank that you are currently banking at. Also, talk to a recommended mortgage broker and see who has the best programs for you.

LOAN TERMS

Down payment: This is simply the amount of money that you are bringing to the table in order to qualify for a loan. A down payment is calculated by the percentage of the purchase price (or the appraised price, whichever is HIGHER). This payment does not include any other fees, liens, etc. that you may be required to pay. For example, if a loan requires a down payment of 10% and the purchase price of the home is $120,000 then your down payment is $120,000 * 0.10 = $12,000.

(To change from a percent to a decimal you simply remove the percent sign and go to the left two spaces for the resulting decimal value. Ex: 12.3% = 0.123; 3.5% = .035; 7% = .07; 130% = 1.30)

Interest Rate: This is the annually based interest rate for the amount of monies borrowed. Your monthly payment is simply that interest rate divided by the 12 months in a calendar year. The interest rate you receive from the bank will be based on some index that the bank borrows the funds plus a value set by the bank for the risk they must take. Risk is evaluated by your credit score and many other factors including your income versus your debt. The most common index that banks borrow is known as LIBOR.

Amortization Schedule: One of the greatest inventions of all time is compound interest. This is how you calculate future values while interest is constantly being put back into the equation. Example, if you have a savings account that pays 5% interest and that interest is re-deposited into your account, then there is a simple formula to account for this constant addition of 5% (which is slightly more after the first interest was deposited after year one which also now gains the interest). The reverse is also true. Every month you are making a payment on a loan (albeit, home or car or other financed object) then a specific amount goes to interest in the first payment (usually the majority of the payment) and a smaller portion goes to the payoff or principal. The second month the payment is the same however a slightly less is going toward the interest and slight more is going toward the principal. This will continue until you are getting toward the end of the loan where the majority of the payment goes to principal and the remaining small portion goes toward interest. This is why you may want to pay additional funds to principal when you can earlier in the loan.

Reserves: This is the amount of capital you have in savings to qualify for a loan. This is after your down payment has been made. The amount in reserves is simply the number of months you could pay the monthly mortgage payment assuming you had no income. Many banks require an additional 3 to 6 months of mortgage payments in savings.

Mid-score: Most loans are determined by your mid, or middle credit score. Thus if you have a 749, a 723, and a 615 score then the number that most banks will use is the 723. They do not average the scores together.

Trade Line: These are lines of credit that you have from an outside source and are reporting to your credit score through one or more of the repositories. These are usually lines of credit like a credit card, car loan, home mortgage loan, or some other form of a loan.

Earnest Money: When you are typically buying a home from the onset the selling person or selling broker wants a form of financial commitment indicating just how serious you are with moving forward. This money is usually refundable only if you, as the buyer, discover something is wrong with the purchase and you back out of the deal prior to a specific date. It may be non-refundable in some other situations or after your inspection period has expired. Earnest money is usually a certified check given with an offer to purchase and is placed in *escrow* once an offer is accepted by both parties. In a lease option this could just be part of the payment you have already paid to the owner or it could just be a $0.

Escrow: This is the process by which you open up an interest in purchasing a home and then all of the mundane dealings that an assortment of people must go through to ensure the transaction is done correctly. "Let's open escrow and purchase this home." This process can take a few weeks to several months depending on each home's situation. Normally if you are buying a home that is a short sale or a foreclosure then you can expect a longer time to actually close on the loan.

Conventional Loan vs. Government Loan

There are two types of Government Loans. It may be easier to view these as bullet points.

- FHA (Federal Housing Administration)
    - More info and updates at www.fha.com.
    - These are government secured loans.
    - May only need a 3.5% down payment.
    - May have to pay a mortgage insurance premium (MIP) if going with a minimal down payment. This is usually a 1.5% upfront fee and an interest rate boost of 0.5% and will last the duration of the loan.
    - Often easier to qualify for than a conventional loan.
    - Minimum of a 620 credit score.
- VA (Veteran's Administration)
    - More info can be found at www.benefits.va.gov/homeloans.
    - For active and retired service people and/or their spouses. As little as 0% down payment.

- o Must qualify as with any other program, i.e., isn't automatically given
- o There is no PMI or MIP.
- o Minimum of a 620 credit score.

Non-government Loans
(1) Conventional Loans
- o Any bank issued loan.
- o If loans are in access of 20% equity position (or 80% financed) then a premium mortgage insurance (PMI) may be enacted by the bank. This is usually the case if you are purchasing a home with only 3% to 5% down payment. This is may or may not be automatically cancelled when your value ratio hits 78%.
- o These are harder to qualify for with less than a 20% down payment.
- o In the past, pre-2005, there were many types of loan programs that the banks were offering. They were given loans to just about anyone, regardless, if the statements made by the borrower were true or not.
- o They were many stated income, stated assets loans (nicknamed "liar loans) were you only stated what your income

or assets were and the bank believed you without any form of verification.

My recommendations is that if you are a veteran or the spouse of a veteran then check out the VA loan first. If you were not a veteran then I would suggest talking to a mortgage broker on both the FHA and conventional loan programs. If you are doing VA or FHA try to find a mortgage broker who specializes in these types of loans.

Mortgage Insurance

Again to cover the different forms of mortgage insurance.

PMI or MIP: This is insurance that you must get on a LOAN if your down payment is less than 20% of the value of the purchase price. This is the bank's insurance policy in the event there is a payment default and they must start to foreclose. *PMI = Private Mortgage Insurance* for conventional loans and *MIP = Mortgage Insurance Premium* for FHA backed loans.

Loan Types:

Interest Only Loan (I.O.): This is a loan that only an interest payment is made. No monies are being applied toward the principal of the loan. This is usually the lowest monthly payment that can be made. However, after the duration of the loan you would have to pay off the entire principal amount or have the home refinanced.

Principle & Interest Loan (P&I): As the name dictates this is a loan that pays both the interest and principal amount based upon an *amortization schedule.* In the beginning most of your monthly payment is going toward interest while only a small portion goes to principal. However, every month a larger portion of the payment goes toward principal. By the end of the loan almost all of your payment is principal and only a small portion is interest.

A loan will be either Interest Only or Principle & Interest.

Loan Rates

Fixed Rate Loan: A fixed rate loan is simply a loan of 15 to 30 years secured by a home that will remain constant for the duration of the loan. This may mean you may have a higher interest rate than an *adjustable rate loan,* however it will never change for the duration of the loan.

Adjustable Rate Loan: These loans are exactly the

opposite of the *fixed rate loan*. What these types of loans offer is an interest rate based on some index and may adjust periodically up or down. In these types of loans usually the first five (5) years are fixed at a constant rate and then starting with the sixth year can adjust. The adjustment is usually based on one of the commercial indexes like the LIBOR. If rates go up, then your payment will go up. If rates go down, your payment goes down. Now this does not happen on a monthly basis, it usually is adjusted annually. Also, there is a fixed percentage that it can go up or down at each adjustment period. Thus, you are capped in the amount of change your loan will undergo at each adjustment period. This can be around 1% change.

Option ARM: These were the loans created back in the early 2000s and in my opinion were one of the causing factors for the mortgage mess we got into. In my personal opinion the option ARM were truly made only for the savvy investor and not the general public.

What these loans do is give you one of four options each month as to what you wanted to pay. The four types of payments sorted by the lowest payment to the highest payment were

    (1) Negative amortization payment;
    (2) Interest Only payment;
    (3) 30 year amortization payment; and

(4) 15 year amortization payment.

Simple crowd mentality dictates that people will usually pay the lowest payment rather than paying the smartest payment. Below are the four choices given further details.

You could pay:
    (1) The lowest payment possible or the "<u>negative amortization payment</u>". This meant you have a loan at 7% yet have the option of pretending it is only a 2% loan and making your payment accordingly. The remainder 5% would simply be added to the tail end of the loan and taken care of 15 - 30 years from now. Your loan amount *increases* every month. Thus, the market must sustain a 5% growth just for the borrower/owner to break even.
    (2) An interest only payment. The next lowest payment amount. This payment assumed you are only paying the 7% interest with nothing applied toward principal.
    (3) A principal and interest payment (P&I) based on a 30 year amortization schedule This is the most common payment people generally would generally pay. This payment is higher than the previous one because you are paying both the interest and then the calculated principal reduction portion.

(4) A principal and interest payment (P&I) based on a 15 year amortization schedule. Since the time frame is cut in half the principal reduction portion has to be doubled (not the interest portion, mind you) to pay off the loan in the shorter time frame.

In my opinion if by some chance you get one of these types of loans I would suggest paying the 30 year amortization payment whenever you can. Thereby, you are actually paying the principal portion off. If times get tough then periodically drop down to the Interest only payment. If you are an investor and happen to have a vacancy on the home this loan is on, then for very brief periods of time take the negative amortization payment, but only if you must. If you have strong cash flow then opt to the 15 year payment to shorten the term of your loan (and the amount of over-all interest you will be paying).

QUALIFYING FOR A LOAN

The following are requirements that a lender will need in order to help you qualify for a loan. This is how they determine how much you can afford.

Debt-to-Income Ratio (DTI): This is one of the

calculations your mortgage person will be using to determine what you can afford or if the home you want is within your budget. The standard DTI to buying a home is 31%. This means your monthly payment (including real estate tax, home owners hazard insurance, home owner association fees, and any other special assessments) must be at 31% of your gross monthly income or less. This is household income for all parties applying for the loan (e.g., a married couple) and not necessarily individual income.

Repository: This is the institution of each of the big three credit reporting agencies (TransUnion, Equifax, and Experian). Each of these reporting agencies have their own formulas in determining you as a credit risk. Many creditors only report to one or two and not all three. Just because you have a default with one credit card does not mean all three *repositories* are going to reflect this. The reason this is so is because a creditor must pay to report to these repositories. Thus, a particular creditor may not want to have that as an expense and feel one or two is enough.

LOAN RESTRICTIONS

The following are restrictions a loan may have. I am only mentioning these here so you are as informed as possible when you are about to sign loan documents or you are discussing your new loan.

Pre-Payment Penalty: A pre-payment penalty is a penalty that you will have to pay if you were to sell or refinance a loan prior to a specific date. These were quite prevalent in the past yet are not as common in today's market. They were enacted so that banks could protect themselves from a borrower paying off a loan too early so they knew the minimum profit a loan would give. Usually, this caused the loan interest rate to drop a small percentage.

Balloon Payment: A balloon payment can be seen in a multitude of ways. It is a set time in the future when all remaining payments on the loan are due at once.

    (1) As an example, you may have a seller who is willing to finance his home to you and wants to keep the payments low so he amortizes it over 30 years. However, he doesn't want to be your bank for the entire 30 years. He may put in a 10 year balloon payment. This would mean that after 10 years of payment, the last payment (120th payment) payment will be the entire rest of the borrowed funds due at.

    (2) Another example is the standard IO (or Interest Only) loan. Ideally, if you got a 20 year IO loan on a home and since no monies are going to reduce principal, at the end of the 20 years the entire purchase price is due.

Rider: This is simply an addendum being added to a loan document. It simply "rides" with the loan.

Grant, Bargain and Sale Deed: This is the best and safest form of transfer of real estate. It guarantees, with insurance, that you are now the rightful owner of the property. If some other claim comes up from the past to rear its ugly head, then you are protected.

Note: This is the actual document giving you the loan. It will state if it is adjustable or fixed rate, the terms of the interest rates (and how they would adjust), the borrowed amount, and the starting and ending dates. This document will be recorded against the title so that future title companies or mortgage brokers can determine what the payoff amount is when you decide to refinance or sell the home.

There are many terms out there that will be specific to a local community that may not have been covered here. Some will include rights to waterways, easements, etc. Just read what the top of each document states and get a brief understanding of what it is. As with the example used in an earlier lesson about a pre-payment rider being inserted, do not hesitate to ask questions or stop the signing process.

Lien: A *lien* is simply a form of interest placed on a property (e.g., a home) to secure a debt that is owed. When you obtain a loan your bank loan will place a *lien* against the property for you. In most all cases, when you buy a home your new loan did pay off all the sellers liens and then is placed in <u>first position</u> as the first lien holder against the home.

DEFAULT TYPES

Since in this day and age many phrases have been floating around for people who have defaulted on their monthly payment. Here is a brief introduction into those terms.

<u>Short Sale</u>: A short sale is when a property owner is in some form of default on the home in which he/she is residing. This only means the home is behind on payments for at least 2 months. What is usually occurring is that the owner of the home is selling the home at a price below the remaining loan amount on the home. This is often due to local market conditions indicate the local area has gone down in value over a period of time. When you are buying a home that is a short sale it means you or your agent will be negotiating with the current bank that has a lien on the property. The seller must sign the proper paperwork, however, they will have very little say to most matters in the contract as that has to be approved by bank committee. Due to this, many short sales take a lot longer time to close than the normal home buying process. Many banks, due to the housing crunch over the past few

years, have put together special departments to only handle short sales thereby making the process more streamlined.

Foreclosed Home (Foreclosure): I want you to pay very close attention to the difference between the words "foreclosure" and "in foreclosure". If a home is "in foreclosure" then that means the seller is still the homeowner. It essentially means a *short sale* (see above) will probably occur. If a property is a "foreclosure" then that means the home is owned by the bank. You will also see the words REO = Real Estate Owned or ORE = Owned Real Estate. This is bank terminology for owning these forms of assets. When dealing with a foreclosure you will be dealing with a bank and bank committee in either case. These, as with a short sale, may take some time. (However, the short sale usually will take longer because the bank may not have worked out what they will accept and then there may be junior liens (like a second mortgage) that also need to be paid.)

Hopefully you didn't get lost with all of the above terms. However you do need to know these as your Realtor, mortgage lender, inspector, and many other parties will be throwing those terms around frequently.

If you are dealing with a lease option many of these terms may not apply to you. However, since you are now in the real estate arena it is good to always have a good understanding as to what is going on. This may have a big effect on your neighborhood so an informed owner is always better off than a person who is not.

Chapter
10

Exercising Your Option

If you are living in a home under a lease option program and you are now ready to buy, now is the time to <u>exercise your option</u>. This means you are now converting the lease option agreement over to a <u>Purchase and Sale Agreement</u>.

If you are in the Western US or a Deed of Trust state then you will be using a title company to do this. If you are in the Eastern US or a Mortgage state then you will need a real estate attorney. There are Deed of Trust states in the East (e.g., North Carolina) and there are Mortgage states in the West (e.g., Arizona). Do a quick internet search to see which is best for your state. All Deed of Trust states have title companies (used solely for purchasing or refinancing a home) and all Mortgage states use a real estate attorneys (they don't usually deal with the purchase of a home). None of the mortgage states have title companies; they only use real estate attorneys.

You start by letting the owner of the home know that you are exercising your option. Then you simply go to the local title office and let them know what you are doing. Most experienced title officers know how to convert a lease option over into a Purchase and Sale contract. The purchase price is known (either from being a set price or you and the owner have agreed on an appraisal value), any credits are also known and the document is drawn up accordingly. Remember these terms are spelled out on the Lease Option Agreement. They will also create what is called a <u>Settlement Statement</u> or <u>HUD-1</u>. This will go into detail the amount of money it is going to cost to close the loan. This will include a variety of things like transfer taxes, proration of property taxes, title searches, etc. This is detailed for both the buyer and the seller.

Once all of these documents are created then the seller will come down to the office to sign his portion of the Purchase and Sale Agreement. Once this is done then you will go over to your mortgage broker to begin the loan process. The title company will do their job also by searching for any liens on the title to the home. The normal process for loan qualification and title work to be done is about 30 days. Be aware that lenders like to close things out by the end of any calendar month. As the last few days approach they are in quick succession to get work done, not only on your deal, but their other deals too. This is not to say your deal will close near the end of the month, it is simply to state there is always a mad dash at the end of the month to close deals, in general.

The process is actually quite an easy one.

At some point in time the bank will have an <u>appraisal</u> done on the home by a <u>certified appraiser</u>. The appraisal is simply an educated guess by the appraiser as to what is the value of the home. If you have already done your homework with your mortgage lender then the appraisal that was done to establish value (assuming you are using the appraised value to determine the purchase price) then that appraisal only needs to be re-certified.

Regardless of how the purchase price was obtained to go into more details on what an appraisal is. The values are determined by comparable matches in the local area to the home you are purchasing. This would be things like lot size, home size, number of bedrooms, etc. Items that do not affect the appraisal would be upgrades inside the home (e.g., granite vs. Formica countertops, tile vs. carpet flooring, stainless steel appliances). Upgrades like patios, pools, etc. will have an effect on the appraisal.

Once the bank approved certified appraiser gives his estimate of the home then that is compared to the purchase price. Quite frequently appraisals come in very close to the purchase price. This is because the appraiser will look at <u>comps</u> or comparable sales to support this purchase price.

Once all is approved by the bank and the title company then you will go down to the title company to sign paperwork. A lot of the other buying process items are not necessarily done when exercising the lease option. A normal buyer would have a due diligence period for inspections and other things to take place. Since you have already been living in the home none of these would be necessary.

There will be a title representative there with you to sign documents. Don't be overwhelmed with the stack of papers you are signing. And there will be a lot of them. You will be signing the note, the deed, any riders or additional items to the note, HOA documents, signature docs, loan docs, etc. The list of documents you are signing is like a small stack. These items will mostly be notarized by the person in the room with you. You will be given a copy of all of these documents (unsigned by anyone) and eventually you will get a copy of the fully signed version.

Within the next couple of days the title company will take the appropriate paperwork down to the country recorder's office to effectively change the ownership of the home. Once the deed is recorded and stamped at the recorder's office then this is called <u>recorded</u>.

When you are working with your lender at the beginning honesty is the best policy. If you lie or misrepresent yourself on the loan documents, at some point in time it will be found out. Therefore, just be honest and then this lender can find you the best deal possible loan with minimal waste of time. If you are dishonest about claims on your credit, or your income, etc. this will probably end up hurting you and your chances of closing the loan. Being honest will make your lender have to search for the creative solutions to your personal predicament.

The lender you work with will need all kinds of documentation. First and foremost is your credit report. Then bank statements for the past 2 months. Proof of employment or w-9 statements if you are employed or income statements of your business (showing write offs) if you are self-employed. Don't fret if they ask for the same documents multiple times. It seems, more frequently than not, that there is a void out at the lending banks that eats documents. You may be required to give updates to bank statements and other forms on a frequent basis.

All-in-all working with your actual mortgage broker should be pleasant, it will just be the bank that you are getting your loan from may be frustrating. This is not to say, all of this unpleasantness will occur, I am just saying don't be surprised if or when it does occur.

Your lender will be pulling your credit report at some time near the start of the process regardless if you have one in hand from another lender or from a credit pulling website. It is their requirements to do this. They will pull your credit again at least one more time toward the end of the process to see if anything has changed during the buying process. NEVER EVER buy a large dollar ticket item during this time. I do not care how attractive the deal may seem. If you have a serious change in your credit profile this may cost you the entire loan. Buying a vehicle, or opening an account with a furniture or electronics store is unwise. Wait until after your loan closes and the deed has been *recorded.* And this includes buying something cash. If your financial bank account changed by $10,000 (for example) then this may cause your reserves don't match their criteria.

Once you get your loan ensure that when you go to sign the closing documents at the title company (the day you get your keys) that the loan you are signing is the one promised you. I know from personal experience when I was doing a refinance on an investment home a few years ago that I specifically said I do not want a pre-payment penalty on the loan because I wanted to have the option of selling or refinancing within the next two or three years. And at the closing table was a <u>Pre-Payment Rider</u> (which a rider just is an addendum that "rides" with the loan) saying I would pay a penalty if I were to refinance or sell the home. I told the title person I am not signing that and had to cancel that signing appointment until the proper documents were submitted. It cost me about 2 or 3 days of time before I was back at the title company signing the appropriate loan, note and associated riders.

Remember these people work for you. You have the final decision in the manner. If there are errors in the paperwork then bring it up. You can always call your mortgage broker while at the signing table.

A word of final caution. The amount of paperwork you will be signing may be overwhelming. Please be aware of what you are signing though. You may not read the documents word for word, however, be aware of what each document represents (like me noticing that rider above).

Now the home is yours.

In the case of Roger and Peggy when they are ready to buy they would simply call Derek and Sue and tell them that they are ready to do so.

Then the process of opening escrow would occur. The title company or real estate attorney would then draft up the purchase contract which all parties sign.

The process moves forward fairly quickly. Since Peggy and Roger already live in the home if there are any delays there is no real issue.

Now you have done everything it takes to qualify and now you are ready to exercise your option. Congratulations!

Lease Options Made Easy – Vol. 1

Chapter 11

Using a Realtor

As mentioned in Chapter 1 there are times that you may not be able to find an investor on your own or that there may not be a local company that specializes in doing lease options. So in these cases you may need to hire a local Realtor to assist you.

Not all Realtors are the same. Most of them deal in one of four areas.
1.) Representing the owner for a rental property. They may also be a certified Property Manager or a Listing Agent.
2.) Representing the owner for a home for sale. This person is known as a Listing Agent.
3.) Representing you as a would-be tenant. This person is the Selling or Renting Agent.
4.) Representing you as a would-be buyer. This is the Selling Agent.

As you can see from the above agents either deal with the selling or renting of the home and may represent either side of the transaction. (In some state they may be able to work on both sides of the transaction.)

Thus, your primary ones will be people who work in the last two categories, primarily the last one.

As you can see most agents are only familiar with buying or selling real estate or the renting of it. Not too many deal with both selling a home and renting the same home at the same time.

If we only focus on the sales side an agent only gets paid by commissions. Thus, when a selling agent helps their client to buy a home when that home closes is when he or she gets paid. However, on a lease option, it may take 1 or more years, if ever, to actually close (meaning you exercise your option and purchase the home). This is why many agents do not want to deal with lease options is due to the timely delays from getting paid.

If you are on your search for this agent (and especially when your agent has to explain your offer to the other agent and seller) find one that is at least open to being creative. As an agent myself when I find a potential lease option tenant/buyer and I don't have a home to personally put them in then I can search the local MLS to help them find a home.

This is what I explain to the other agent. This way the financial motivations for all parties are addressed. The reason for this is that when people don't understand something when an offer or opportunity is presented then they almost always answer "no".

Thus, I suggest you tell your agent is to explain the offer this way. Number one on commissions will be paid out by splitting the option payment into three. One third goes to the owner, one-third to the selling agent's broker, and one-third to your buyers agent's broker. Then when the option is exercised in the future then the full remaining portion of the commission is paid to all parties.

The reason this works a lot better is that everyone is getting paid more than just renting the home and there is a future incentive to both agents, especially the buyer's agent to assist you in getting your credit to the point that you can purchase the home.

It is always nice as being either agent to all of a sudden hear that a deal that was done a year or so ago is now going to pay out a second time. And everyone is happy.

You are happy as you get the home of your dreams.

Both agents got their commissions.

And the owner not only got his sales price he was asking he got a lot more profit from the monthly rental payments.

Can someone say "Win!".

Chapter
12

Pros and Cons on a Lease Option

Just as there are good parts of a lease option there are also the negative or the con side of doing a lease option. The biggest downside is the number of people who actually exercise their options. In the many years that I have done these I would say only about 10% actually end up buying the home. The main reason that I see is that the tenant/buyer never actually gets his or her credit up to point to purchase or they just end up changing their minds.

Nothing is sadder to my eyes is seeing someone decide to just leave the home. There are techniques, (ideally investor techniques that we will cover in Vol. 3) that a tenant/buyer could use to get back their investment and could even make a profit.

All that I can say is that you are well informed before putting your money down on a home for a lease option. Make sure it is the home you eventually do want to buy.

About the Author

To start I want to tell you about the journey I led so that you can get to know more about me and where I come.

I grew up in a very small town a few miles outside the city of Pensacola, FL. My parents divorced in 1977 (near my 10th birthday) and I grew up predominately with my mom.

As with many small town kids growing up in a divorced home back in the 1980's and early 1990's I focused on other things. I was fairly academic in school. I was the average A-B student (*my little brother being solitarian in the class one year after mine*).

After High School I joined the Navy for nearly 5 years and was able to see a lot of the world. I was stationed in Japan for 4 years and was able to see a lot of Asia and Australia. After the Navy I used my G.I. Bill and went to college receiving a Bachelor's of Arts degree in Applied Mathematics with a minor in Psychology. I then attended FSU (Florida State University) in 1994 to study Physical Meteorology (the mathematics of weather patterns). I stayed there for an entire three years as a

About the Author

full time student yet didn't quite finish my Master's Degree.

I got hired on to do many other jobs over the next few years. First of all was a computer programmer (since I did a lot of programming for my major at FSU) for the Y2K project starting in 1997 – 1999. Then got downsized after that project and went into my first self-employed opportunity / network marketing business. This led to being hired on as a college math teacher in North Carolina. While there I was introduced to books like *Rich Dad, Poor Dad* by Robert Kiyosaki and audio programs like *Personal Power* by Tony Robbins.

This is how I got into real estate in January of 2002. After reading about the four quadrants I knew I had to get into real estate and do it fast. I ended buying two houses which eventually led into buying a small apartment complex in Alabama.

During 2003 I was introduced to a man named Eric that was a coach with the Rich Dad organization and he was telling me just how hot the real estate market was in Las Vegas. And that I had to get out there. I took him up on his word. Eric had formed partnerships with 5 other people to set up an investment company in Las Vegas where they would buy homes in foreclosure or short sale (a very hard product to come by since homes were appreciating wilding at that time in Las Vegas). He told me to give him a call when I was ready to come out.

About the Author

In late 2003 I made the decision to quit my job as a bartender at a beach bar in Carolina Beach, NC and also quit both of my teaching jobs at two local community colleges. I was going to take a leap of faith and move across the country to Las Vegas and try my hand at real estate investing. I sold everything that would not fit in a 4'x8' U-Haul trailer (the smallest one they had that a four cylinder Toyota pickup truck could carry across the mountains of the country) and prepared for my move.

One lucky thing was that when I was preparing to move I stayed with different friends. Both of my homes were in Wilmington were in the process of being rented so I could not live there. I slept on my friend Pam's couch for over a month around the Thanksgiving holiday of 2003. A friend of mine took Pam out to dinner one night and I realized after his return from dropping her off at her home that he was moving out to Las Vegas in December 2003 and he already had a job there. I told him I will be there the following month! Wow what a coincidence! A friend that was taking my then roommate out to dinner was moving to Vegas one month prior to me moving out to Vegas. I love you Mike!

In January 2004 I loaded up my truck and U-Haul and headed away from the beach of NC.

As I was approaching Arizona I began to get a little nervous. My contacts for whom I was moving across the country for still had not returned my calls. I am now

About the Author

about 1 day away of arriving and they don't know I am coming. While driving along I-40 I found another number for the group. This happen to be a round robin telephone number. It so happen that nobody answered. So I left a message. I am now about 4 hours away from arriving. When I was near Kingman, AZ I got a call from Eric asking where I was. I told him I am about an hour away from Hoover Damn (which is just south of Las Vegas). He said to call him when I was closer.

I recall coming up from the south of Las Vegas for my first time ever in this city. The lights were amazing as I was coming in from the South. I called Eric stating I was in town and he gave me the directions to find the home they were house sitting.

I started working with Eric and his crew for a few months until they could not agree on which strategy to partake and they eventually disbanded in June 2004, just 6 short months after my arrival.

At that time I was desperate to find a source of income to support myself. Somehow, I don't recall how, I met up for lunch with the first person whom would become my first lease option partner, Michelle Larson, and a new business was formed that would lead to many people becoming home owners in the future.

She was a Nevada Realtor and I was new to being a connector type of investor. After leaving the disbanded group that Eric belonged, I had a huge network of investors who wanted to buy in Vegas.

About the Author

Since homes were appreciating in the 40-50% per year, we created an unique program. We found people who could not qualify for a home and had them start looking at homes for sale on the MLS until they found one they liked. I would then write an offer on those homes until one was accepted. I would then quickly assign my interest to another investor who would actually purchase the home for that would-be buyer. The would-be buyer would move in on a one year contract, with the possibly ability to extend as necessary.

In 2005 Michelle and I would approach an impasse that we could not resolve and we disbanded our relationship. I continued to move forward with the same concept with my second Realtor partner, Mesha. We did a number of deals until she found more lucrative possibilities elsewhere. At this time the housing market began to shift quite strong. Homes in Las Vegas were no longer appreciating, they were actually dropping dramatically. Over the course of the next few years many homes dropped by nearly 50% or more.

Investors, including myself, lost tons of money in real estate. Many investors went bankrupt.

As times changed, so did the lease option program. We had to adjust for the times. We no longer offered the program of tenant/buyers being able to buy off of the MLS. We could only deal with those people who would buy from investors that already had homes available. Thus, in 2006 we adjusted our program to close to what

About the Author

it is today. We now work with tenant/buyers in looking at our current inventory and then if those don't work out then we search the MLS and try to find them on there (much like Chapter 11 states).

Printed in Poland
by Amazon Fulfillment
Poland Sp. z o.o., Wrocław